"It's here that Massicotte is at his most graceful
and amiable as a writer."
—Kamal Al-Solaylee, *The Globe and Mail*

"Massicotte's script is marvellous writing. It presents their ironic
rebellion of practical jokes at Oxford as unfolding in parallel with
the global consequences of the Arab rebellion, questioning the
extent and intent of Lawrence's personal and political
manipulations (as genuine scholarship does) and showing Graves
trying to piece together a semblance of family life. Massicotte's
play delivers an effective and affecting performance that, when
one considers the present military adventures, elicits
a return to Graves' question: 'After the War?'"
—Jeremy Mesiano-Crookston, *Ottawa Xpress*

"In *The Oxford Roof Climber's Rebellion*, playwright
Stephen Massicotte combines historical fact and
a measure of his own fiction to powerful effect."
—John Coulbourn, *Toronto Sun*

"The script has some fine moments, mostly in depicting the
relationship between the complex, ironic, self-flagellating
Lawrence and the emotionally hemmed-in Graves,
who is suffering from survivor's guilt."
—Jon Kaplan, *NOW* Magazine

"Canadian playwright Stephen Massicotte has taken on the
enormously ambitious task of casting a new gaze on the much
written about lives of T.E. Lawrence and poet Robert Graves. His
play is a fascinating study of the effects of trauma on these men
who were literary landmarks of the 20th Century. …
Crisp, intelligent, witty, ironic and at times very moving
dialogue, a text that flows blithely on without ever appearing
pedantic or overly written, in spite of the weight of
the literary characters it portrays."
—Alvina Ruprecht, CBC "Ottawa Morning"

The *Oxford Roof Climber's* REBELLION

THE OXFORD ROOF
CLIMBER'S REBELLION

STEPHEN MASSICOTTE

Playwrights Canada Press
Toronto • Canada

The Oxford Roof Climber's Rebellion
© Copyright 2006 Stephen Massicotte
The moral rights of the author are asserted.

Playwrights Canada Press
The Canadian Drama Publisher
215 Spadina Ave., Suite 230, Toronto, Ontario CANADA M5T 2C7
416.703.0013   fax 416.408.3402
orders@playwrightscanada.com • www.playwrightscanada.com

Financial support provided by the taxpayers of Canada and Ontario through the Canada Council for the Arts and the Department of Canadian Heritage through the Book Publishing Industry Development Programme, and the Ontario Arts Council.

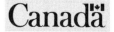 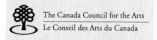

Cover photo by S. Massicotte: Bust of T. E. Lawrence, Jesus College Chapel, Oxford.
Production Editor: MZK

Library and Archives Canada Cataloguing in Publication

Massicotte, Stephen
   The Oxford roof climber's rebellion / Stephen Massicotte.

A play.

ISBN 978-0-88754-499-6

   1. Lawrence, T. E. (Thomas Edward), 1888-1935 – Drama.
   2. Graves, Robert,

1895-1985--Drama. 3. World War, 1914-1918--Drama. I. Title.

PS8576.A79668O95 2007   C812'.6   C2007-902964-7

First edition: May 2007.
Printed and bound by Canadian Printco at Scarborough, Canada.

•SPECIAL THANKS & ACKNOWLEDGMENTS•

The Oxford Roof Climber's Rebellion (ORCR) was commissioned by the National Arts Centre of Canada, English Theatre. It was developed with the assistance of The Alberta Playwrights' Network's Fresh Ink Festival, Theatre Alliance's Pangaea Project and Theatre Junction's Random Acts Festival.

I would like to acknowledge the support of Marti Maraden, Maureen Labonte, Vanessa Porteous, Jeremy Skidmore, Colleen Murphy, Grant Harvey, Ian Prinsloo, Iris Turcott, the Robert Graves Estate, the Canadian Stage Company, Vertigo Theatre, the Globe Theatre, the Vancouver Playhouse, the University of British Columbia, the Thunder Bay Public Library and the Canadian Embassy in Washington DC.

The ORCR was researched with the assistance of Deirdre Arthur, Dara Price (whose bicycle was stolen in the service of the play), Corrina and Robert Gaussen, Jesus College – Oxford, All Soul's College, the Imperial War Museum – London, the National Portrait Gallery – London, St. Paul's Cathedral, the Ashmolean Museum of Art and Archaeology, the Tank Museum – Bovington, St Martin's Church - Wareham, Cloud's Hill – The National Trust and the Wareham Town Museum.

My sincere admiration and appreciation goes to Lise Ann Johnson, Richard Rose, the Tarragon Theatre and the Great Canadian Theatre Company for bringing the Oxford Roof Climbers, the Benevolant Order of, to life. Thank you to the actors who lent their voices to the play during its development; Mark Bellamy, Kira Bradley, Ben Carlson, Jayne Collins, Ralph Cosham, Bob Fraser, Donna Goodman, Jim Hobson, Christopher Hunt, Alex Jecchinis, Harry Judge, Richard Kenyon, Michael Kramer, Nicole Leroux, Jim Leyden, Erin Moon, Casie Platt, Greg Schneider, Jason Schneider, Tanya Schneider, Jason Stiles and Alexander Strain.

Last but not least, I'd like to thank my brother Joel for introducing me to "Lawrence of Arabia." He brought the video of the David Lean film home to Thunder Bay from a high school trip to Victoria. Shortly thereafter the copy of T. E. Lawrence's *The Seven*

Pillars of Wisdom went missing from the library of Sir Winston Churchill C. & V. I. That book was later found on the bookshelf in the room that I shared with my brother. Regardless of how it got there I do apologize to and thank the librarian at that time, Mr. Peet. It was the dedicatory poem in the *Seven Pillars* that inspired my first piece of creative writing in August of 1992. I print my awkward and highly derivative poem here because it is unlikely to be published anywhere else:

THE FALL TO HILLS

The brave heart strives and paints
its name across the heavens
for hope that its valour will etch its place.

For love and hate and laughter
its mark across it leaves
by will and honour to leave a sign.

To smile and move with purpose it strives
to fight the shifting sands
that cover and move swiftly.

We hope and pray by claw or tooth
to cling a little, a little longer.

For time passes and mountains fall to hills and with them
the brave heart gasps and prays to be held
and to be remembered.

—SM

There are nine hundred and ninety-nine patrons of virtue to one virtuous man.

—Henry David Thoreau, *Civil Disobedience*

Wisdom has built her house. She hath hewn out her seven pillars.

—*Proverbs 9:1*

I loved you, so I drew these tides of men into my hands and wrote my will across the sky with stars.

—T. E. Lawrence, *The Seven Pillars of Wisdom*

The Oxford Roof Climber's Rebellion was first produced as a co-production between the Great Canadian Theatre Company and the Tarragon Theatre from October to December 2006 with the following company:

Captain Robert Graves	Jonathan Crombie
Colonel T. E. Lawrence (of Arabia), Ned	Tom Rooney
Jack Dawkins	Paul Rainville
Lord George Nathaniel Curzon	Victor Ertmanis
Nancy Nicholson	Michelle Giroux

Directed by Richard Rose
Set and Costume Design by Charlotte Dean
Lighting Design by Graeme S. Thompson
Sound Design by Todd Charlton
Stage Manager: Kathryn Westoll
Apprentice Stage Manager: Tara Tomlinson
Dramaturg: Lise Ann Johnson

• **Playwright's Note** •

Although throughout the play the Oxford Roof Climbers' Rebellion is identified as plural, it will be found in scene seven that the singular usage on the cover—Climber's Rebellion—is not only appropriate but fitting.

> *An Oxford University garden, one evening in 1920.*
> *ROBERT Graves, 24, a man with dark curly hair, in*
> *formal attire, is found on stage, holding his handkerchief*
> *to his mouth. He is trembling with the bout of coughing*
> *he is trying to stifle. Thomas Edward Lawrence (NED),*
> *33, a man with fair hair, also in formal evening dress*
> *enters with a bunch of grapes in his hands. He wipes*
> *each grape individually with his own handkerchief before*
> *eating them. A servant, JACK Dawkins 55, stands*
> *discreetly to one side.*

NED   That is an impressive lack of cough you have there.

ROBERT   I'm fine. Shrapnel. Hardly enough to fuss over. Hit twice slightly in the left hand and was running back in rushes through Bazentin Cemetery to avoid some accurate artillery. An eight-inch shell hit behind me about three paces. A piece through here.

> *Points to his thigh, high up, near his groin. NED*
> *whistles in reaction to the proximity of ROBERT's*
> *wound.*

I took a chip of marble off a grave stone in the forehead and another split my finger bone.

NED   And the lung?

ROBERT   A piece below my right shoulder blade and came out here.

> *A point two inches above his right nipple.*

It looked so bad the surgeons put me amongst the dead. It was duly reported home that I'd "Died of Wounds." Then I sat up and they said "this bloke's not dead" and by the time I got home I was able to read my obituary in the *Times*. Now I wonder if parts of me stayed dead.

> *ROBERT's coughing has passed. His hands are again*
> *steady.*

It's much better now, see?

NED   You know, I read a book of yours in 1917 and thought it quite good.

ROBERT   That's very kind of you to say. Have we met?

NED   How did it go? "What life to lead and where to go After the War, after the War?"

ROBERT   Ah, *Over the Brazier*. That is how it goes. Exactly.

NED   "What life to lead and where to go
After the War, after the War?
I'd thought: 'A cottage in the hills,
North Wales, a cottage full of books,
Pictures and brass and cosy nooks
And comfortable broad windowsills,
Flowers in the garden, walls all white.
I'd live there peacefully and dream and write.'"

ROBERT   Precisely. Thank you. Please don't do that again. You have me at a disadvantage.

NED   It's a habit of mine.

ROBERT   Reciting poetry or having the advantage?

NED   Oh, must I pick between the two? They're both very helpful at parties like this one. If you find yourself in an uncomfortable situation, you simply begin reciting something from memory with a mystical look in your eye and you'll quickly find yourself blissfully alone.

ROBERT   You weren't raving to shake hands with Lord Curzon?

NED   I'm the newest Fellow of All Soul's College and since this is All Soul's, attendance was nearly mandatory. What's your excuse?

ROBERT   I'm just a guest tonight of my father's.

NED   Aren't we all.

> *JACK whistles to warn of the entrance of a stately man with cane and evening clothes. Purely Victorian, about 61 years old.*

NED & ROBERT   Oh, bloody hell.

NED and ROBERT look for an escape but there isn't one.

CURZON Ah, Colonel Lawrence, getting a breath of fresh air, or a breath of fresh admirer? Colonel Lawrence likes his admirers one at a time, so that they can't compare notes.

ROBERT Thomas Edward Lawrence?

NED Oh, do call me Ned, if you like. Lawrence of Arabia is so very tedious don't you find? Since that show about him is selling out in the West-End, he's received letters from as far away as America, Canada, and even Japan, requesting the usual things, to be the godfather to their children, to speak at universities. Marriage.

CURZON Hmph.

NED Oh, yes, it's quite unsettling. Twenty-three offers and counting.

ROBERT Why don't you get them to pull the show?

NED I've seen it nine times. It's wonderful. I could see about tickets?

CURZON Lord George Nathaniel Curzon.

> *CURZON holds out his hand to ROBERT who takes it.*

ROBERT Your Lordship.

NED Introductions, yes. Former Viceroy of India, former Member of the War Cabinet, former drinker of champagne at the Treaty of Versailles in 1919. Zero offers of marriage.

ROBERT Robert Graves. Poet.

NED Captain, retired, survivor of the Battle of the Somme.

CURZON Always a pleasure to make the acquaintance of a soldier.

NED Shrapnel through the lung. Finger. Thigh. Finger. Finger. Forehead.

ROBERT Congratulations, my Lord, on your appointment to Vice Chancellor of Oxford University.

l to r: Tom Rooney, Jonathan Crombie, Victor Ertmanis, Paul Rainville.
Photo by Cylla von Tiedemann.

CURZON   For the most part an honourary title so I can continue to devote myself to the Foreign Office. I am not yet the Former Foreign Secretary.

NED   A crime.

CURZON   You'll have to forgive Colonel Lawrence. We really are old friends.

ROBERT   That is quite evident.

NED   We really are.

CURZON   How long has it been, Colonel?

NED   A little less than a year. Seems barely a week ago doesn't it?

CURZON   The crown is grateful to you for encouraging the Arab tribes to rise up and overthrow their Turkish masters. Your efforts played a significant role in defeating Germany and isn't that what we all fought for?

NED   I blew up a few Turkish trains.

CURZON   In Paris, you fervently pleaded the case for Arab independence, admirably one might even add, but the Treaty of Versailles wasn't convinced. The French have Syria and we have Mesopotamia, which we will dutifully shepherd into the fold. Prince Feisel's Arabia was a dream but we all know the stuff that dreams are made on.

ROBERT   What are your dreams made on, your Lordship?

CURZON   Why, for the most part sleep.

> *NED baas like a lamb.*

But now that you've done with king-making, and king-making is done with you, it's quite nice to see your familiar face so comfortably ensconced here in academia.

NED   Yes, some powerful friends recommended I retire from active service and accept a seven-year Fellowship here at All Soul's to write my book.

CURZON   Seven years of peace and quiet. How could you refuse such a generous offer?

> *ROBERT can't help but scoff.*

NED   Oh, I was quite eager to write my account of the Arab Revolt against the Turkish Empire and the events that led us here... to this very moment.

CURZON   Seven years is a long time, do save some of it for the end.

NED   Was there some reason you came calling, Lord Curzon?

CURZON   Yes, my visit wasn't merely cordial. To commemorate the first anniversary of the Armistice, I am working to set aside a permanent memorial to the Great War.

NED   A statue or a plaque?

CURZON   A day. Throughout the Commonwealth memorial services will be held annually on the 11th to honour the glorious dead so their sacrifice will never be forgotten.

NED   A day of remembrance? I see.

CURZON   Being that you served, are well spoken and popular, I would like to officially request you speak at services being prepared by the Bishop of Oxford at Christ Church Cathedral.

NED   What would you like me to remember?

CURZON   Those who laid down their lives for King and Country.

NED   I once had a camel whose lineage ran nine generations. Ghazala, tall as a ship. She gave birth to a lovely foal but it died. Ghazala folded up her legs like ladders. Her eyes soaked out onto her face like deep wells in the sand. She would not, could not get up, and no other camel would unless she did. One day before we set out to destroy a train, my man Abdullah fetched out the dead foal's hide, which he'd skinned and dried. He lay it out in front of Ghazala. He whispered to her as she nuzzled the square. *Adees sarlik hoon, Ghazala? Tfaddali mai.* And she clambered up and there was a great roar as they all rumbled and rose. And we did twelve miles like that or thirty before she remembered, then lowered her knees and lay down again. Abdullah ran out the foal's hide and again he whispered. *Adees sarlik hoon, Ghazala? Tfaddali mai.* How long are you going to lie here, Ghazala? Come along with me please. She rose up and we rode on. Three times we did this. Then we never needed the foal again.

ROBERT   A parable about forgetting?

NED   A parable for camels. No. I am not at all interested.

CURZON   And you haven't spoken to Feisal?

NED   Not since that night of goodbyes on the Eiffel tower.

> *NED waves a romantic farewell with his handkerchief.*

CURZON   Oh, I see, you truly are retired then.

> *NED waves the handkerchief in surrender.*

NED   Yes, truly.

CURZON   Well then, do enjoy the term, Lawrence. Captain.

NED   Lord Curzon, if I was in charge of a regiment and you were in charge of a regiment, I know which one of us would be taken prisoner first.

CURZON   And I know which one of us would talk his way out of it.

CURZON exits back in to the party.

NED   The peerage always have the last word. It's inherited.

ROBERT   It's a bloody miracle in all those years with all those bullets flying around that a few of them didn't find their way towards men like him.

NED   It's no use. Men like him have very thick desks.

ROBERT   I say form the firing squads. Cut all the Union Jacks into blindfolds.

NED   Line up the guilty? I think we start that, we'll find there are not nearly enough bullets for the job.

ROBERT   No more bullets by the millions. We saw what that accomplishes. I have a new theory about bullets. One is all it'll take. It simply has to be aimed in the right direction. Bloody great criminals like Curzon.

NED   "Home's played out:
Old England's quite a hopeless place,
I've lost all feeling for my race:
The English stay-at-home's a tout
A cad; I've done with him for my life."

ROBERT   That's twice you've quoted me. If you do it again I'll have to shoot you. All we talked about was the clean sweep we were going to make of the politicians and generals that sent us out there and now we've come home there's not a peep to be heard. Oxford is full of us, officers and men, fresh from hell, nose in the books. You yourself are our most distinguished retiree? And here you are hiding from Curzon in the garden.

l to r: Tom Rooney, Jonathan Crombie.
Photo by Cylla von Tiedemann.

NED   I'm not hiding in the garden. I'm hiding in the garden with you.

ROBERT   A pair of Adams.

NED   That would have saved the world a lot of trouble.

ROBERT   Well, I should go back inside. My father will be wanting to introduce me to someone.

NED   I suppose, then, I'll just have to climb that roof by myself.

ROBERT   I beg your pardon?

NED   Growing up in Oxford, we ruled the roofs of this place. We had a secret society. My brothers and I, well not Arny the little worm, he was too small. We called ourselves the Oxford Roof Climbers, the Benevolent Order of.

> *NED salutes in the manner of the Benevolent Order. A salute of opposites, executed with a swoop of the right hand to the side of the left brow, palm up.*

Magdalen College, the Ashmolean Museum, the Sheldonian Theatre. The only one we never managed was the ascent up the dome of the Radcliffe Camera. That was all a thousand years ago, sometimes even longer.

ROBERT   Awfully dangerous.

NED   Awfully is my favourite kind.

ROBERT   Do you still climb?

NED   It's awfully dangerous.

ROBERT   It's your favourite kind.

> *NED, taking the dare, hands his jacket to JACK.*

NED   Thank you, Jack.

> *NED moves to climb the wall leading up to the roof. ROBERT moves to help him reach his first hold.*

No thank you, I can't bear to be touched. It's nothing personal. Actually, it's entirely personal but not at all your fault.

> *ROBERT removes his jacket and then takes his own first handholds on the wall. NED is already climbing.*

Where in God's name do you think you're going, young man?

ROBERT   I've done some climbing in Wales.

NED   Ah... you're a standing member of the Oxford Roof Climbers, the Benevolent Order of?

ROBERT   No... but...

NED   Oh, come on then but we'll have to have an initiation. Teach you the secret birdcall. Bree-oo, bree-oo, bree-oop. You'll have to pray all night over your weapons and armour before you fetch me the cup of Christ.

> *NED climbs out of sight and ROBERT follows him up the wall. NED can be heard singing from off.*

A lovely black eye has my Uncle Jim
Somebody threw a tomato at him
Tomatoes don't hurt I said with a grin
Ah yes, they do when they're still in the tin.
Bree-oo, bree-oo, bree-oop.

> *ROBERT climbs out of sight, up onto the roofs of All Soul's.*

• • II • •

> *Night. Graves' home, Dingle Cottage, several weeks later. ROBERT enters, coming home with some Arab clothes under his arm.*

NANCY   *(off)* Robert, are you down there?

> *ROBERT crosses over and sits at the table. He pretends that he has been working on some poetry. NANCY enters, tying a robe around her.*

ROBERT   I've woken you.

NANCY   You thought you were being quiet.

ROBERT   Yes, I thought I was.

NANCY   Not quiet enough to keep secrets from me.

ROBERT   The dew was settling as I walked up the hill.

NANCY   It's this cottage. It's damp. You didn't come to bed?

ROBERT   I did.

NANCY   I didn't hear you.

ROBERT   Well, I almost did.

NANCY   What kept you?

ROBERT   You. Right before I got into bed I got caught up in looking at you sleeping. Your hair, the breath on your lips, your pink cheeks…

> *He gives her a kiss.*

NANCY   Liar. My cheeks are really quite pale and sometimes a sort of greenish. It's how you tell the young mothers from the newlyweds.

ROBERT   I'm sorry I left you alone with the children.

NANCY   Another late evening with Ned?

> *NANCY finds the Arab robe and headgear lying on chair.*

ROBERT   Yes, we lost track of the time.

NANCY   Playing dress up?

ROBERT   Ah, those are mine. He gave them to me. You can't look at a single one of his possessions without him wanting to give them to you. Here, let me show you.

> *ROBERT takes up the head-cloth and agal to model them for her. He wraps the head-cloth around his head.*

This one goes on like this.

> *He then secures the cloth by crowning himself with the agal ropes.*

And this one like a crown. *Assalam alaika.*

NANCY   I beg your pardon?

ROBERT   Peace be upon you.

NANCY   And what am I to say to that?

ROBERT   *Wa alaika assalam.*

NANCY   Dib dib dob.

ROBERT   And also with you. Don't I look dashing?

NANCY   Graves of Arabia. Oh, ha, I've made a pun.

> *ROBERT removes the head-cloth and hangs it on the back of a chair and goes back to pretending to write. NANCY takes up the Arab robes and tries them on over her own.*

Like something out of the Arabian Nights; a regular Ali Baba. You did look dashing. It's lovely silk. Is this silver thread?

ROBERT   The robes of a Prince of Mecca.

NANCY   He just gave them to you?

ROBERT   Yes, just said have them or I'll throw them away.

NANCY   Why would he do such a thing?

ROBERT   Why particularly not?

NANCY   He doesn't seem the kind that does anything without a calculated reaction.

ROBERT   What sort of reaction did you have in mind?

NANCY   Well, you know he turned down the knighthood in the presence of the King.

ROBERT   You little gossip.

NANCY   If he wanted to simply decline the honour, couldn't he just have written a polite letter? But he went right in to Buckingham Palace, let the King take the DSO and the Order of the Bath from the cushion and at that moment refused them.

ROBERT   What's wrong with that?

NANCY   What's wrong with that? It seems to me he didn't want to take the medals home, but he certainly wanted to receive them.

ROBERT   I don't know, Nancy, do you want me to ask him?

NANCY   Would you?

ROBERT   We don't talk of such things.

NANCY   What do you talk about?

ROBERT   Oh, Meleager's influence on St. James' Epistle, Ezra Pound's essays on Imagist poetry and Roman Emperors with stutters.

NANCY   Poetry, excellent. Are you getting any of it down?

ROBERT   I was just sitting down to do so.

> *NANCY removes the Arab robes and overlooks ROBERT's writing.*

NANCY   Where's the rest of it?

ROBERT   I left it with Ned, for proofing.

NANCY   I thought I was your proofer?

ROBERT   I thought that it might be nice to have another eye.

NANCY   They say Lawrence clapped for service at Fuller's Tea Shop the other day.

ROBERT   That's what they do in the Middle East.

NANCY   But this is Oxford, in England, and in Oxford and in England one can cause quite a little scandal by clapping for service in the Middle Eastern fashion.

> *NANCY claps twice.*

ROBERT   One can also cause quite the little scandal by wearing male fashion when one is a young mother.

NANCY   Perhaps I should dream up something a bit more shocking then?

ROBERT   Oh, what could you do?

NANCY   I'll shave my head.

ROBERT   No, not that, you're such a lovely boy.

NANCY   For every true English homosexual, there are ten by default. It's the school system. The lamentable lack of females. All that football and rugger. The walking arm in arm. Oh, come now, Robert, you walked arm in arm. You and your mates?

ROBERT   You could go on like that at Fuller's Tea Shop. That would cause a scandal.

NANCY   I am not playing, Robert.

ROBERT   I didn't think you were. You know, you and Lawrence have a lot in common?

NANCY   Did you mean country matters?

ROBERT   Don't be lewd. You both like to make a show of stirring the pot.

NANCY   Do you think my behaviour affected? My hair, the children not being christened, socialism? I do these things for one reason.

> Upstairs, one of the children stirs. NANCY and ROBERT listen to hear if the baby wakes.

ROBERT   To drive my mother to distraction.

NANCY   I do these things for our children. And to drive your mother to distraction.

ROBERT   It's going to take more than you riding a boy's bicycle past some outraged Jesus College dons to save our children.

NANCY   We each fight our battles our own way, don't we?

ROBERT   Some of us fought our battles on battlefields.

NANCY   This is a new kind of fight in a new kind of battle for a new kind of victory.

ROBERT   I'm not sure I know how to fight it.

NANCY   You'll write your rhymes and I'll illustrate them and we'll put out our children's books and we'll sell many copies and we'll be happy. You know? How we planned? How is it coming, hmm?

ROBERT   My father said he'd help us out.

NANCY   We mustn't take your father's money.

ROBERT   I wish you wouldn't say "Father's" like that.

NANCY   We mustn't take his money.

ROBERT   He's offered.

NANCY   Their England is finished and if there's to be a new one, we must make it. And we cannot make it if we owe them everything.

ROBERT   We'll have to let go of the nanny.

NANCY   Then we give her the sack and we do it ourselves.

ROBERT   I think there may be, I think there is something wrong with me.

NANCY   Nonsense. It's just too much at once, that's all. Your studies, the children, the shop, the damp.

ROBERT   The war—

NANCY   I don't want the war in my house – our house. We promised we wouldn't have it here. We promised to make a new world. You don't have to do it alone. I will help you. And when we're better, England will be better.

ROBERT   Yes.

NANCY   Yes. It's almost morning. Almost time to open shop. You write some more poetry, poet. You're behind the counter this afternoon.

> *ROBERT continues to make it look like he's writing.*

ROBERT   Go to bed.

NANCY   With the two wee ones there's so precious little quiet it's a shame to waste it sleeping.

> *NANCY flirtatiously takes the pencil from ROBERT's hand and makes as if to lead him to the bedroom. Then there is crying from one of the children. NANCY lets go of ROBERT's hands and goes upstairs. ROBERT shivers and looks up at the sky through the roof. He seems to be hearing artillery explosions that no one else can hear. He covers his head with his hands and tries to plug his ears. ROBERT crawls under the table and curls up in ball.*

ROBERT   Oh, God... oh, God, please... please make it stop... please... please...

NANCY   *(off)* There, there, good morning little David.

> *The second baby joins in on the crying.*

Oh, and you too, pretty Jenny? Good morning to you too, sweetness... Robert? Could you be a dear?

> *An artillery shell whistles in and the explosion seems to shatter the cottage.*

••III••

> *NED's room at All Soul's is covered in blank writing paper and a crumpled newspaper. On his table is his typewriter and a tea service. NED is in a dishevelled state and hasn't slept. He is standing on the window ledge and ringing a brass train station bell out the window. In his other hand NED brandishes his Webley service revolver. JACK, NED's servant, is trying to calm NED down.*

JACK   But, sir, it's just past six in the morning, you'll wake the whole college.

NED   Good, it needs a good waking up.

> *He rings the bell some more.*

JACK   Sir, please, do come in from there—

NED   I've told you a hundred times, Jack, I'm no longer a sir.

JACK   Have it your way, sir, but please come in, I'll fetch you a toasted scone. You know how you like your toasted scones, sir?

> *NED rings the bell.*

NED   Hear ye, hear ye. The world is run by liars and cheats. Don't believe a word of any of it.

JACK   Sir, sir, someone will call the constabulary.

NED   I'll be out in under an hour. I have powerful friends.

> *Again, he rings the bell. ROBERT comes running in, some books in hand.*

ROBERT   What in God's name are you doing?

NED   Oh, it's you. Up bright and early and ready for school?

ROBERT   What's that you've got there in your hand?

NED   I *liberated* this from Tel Shawm station. I'm tolling it as loud as I can. I can't sleep so why should they?

ROBERT   Your other hand?

NED   Oh, this old thing? Don't you recognize it? You were in the army, didn't they issue you a service revolver?

ROBERT   What are you doing with it?

NED   Isn't it obvious? I'm waving it around the room willy-nilly.

ROBERT   I can see that, but why?

NED   I don't want to talk about it.

ROBERT   Let's don't then. Just come in from the window. You'll fall.

NED   I shall not fall. I have willpower.

ROBERT   You keep willpower. I'll have gravity.

l to r: Tom Rooney, Jonathan Crombie.
Photo by Cylla von Tiedemann.

ROBERT steps towards NED. NED points his revolver at him.

NED Don't touch me. Don't.

ROBERT I haven't. I won't.

NED Just, please, stay where you are.

ROBERT You... you really can't bear to be touched can you?

NED I said as much. You thought I was joking? Well, I wasn't.

NED slowly lowers his revolver.

I'm sorry, I had no right to point this thing at you. You were never in any danger. I keep it loaded with blanks.

JACK He was up all night, sir, trying to write, then I brought him his tea and the morning papers and he just, well, you can see for yourself, sir.

ROBERT Why don't you come out of there and have a cup of tea?

NED   The tea's cold.

JACK   Shall I fetch a fresh pot, sir?

ROBERT   Do, Jack, please.

JACK   Right away, sir.

> *JACK gathers up the tea service and exits. ROBERT picks up the crumpled newspaper unfolds it and reads the headline.*

ROBERT   "The Emir Feisal Declares Sovereignty in Syria."

NED   French Forces seize Damascus and declare martial law. British Army likewise enforce curfew in Baghdad.

ROBERT   I see. Perhaps if Feisal withdraws, an escalation can be avoided.

NED   I doubt it. Violence is a fire that feeds on retaliation. Curzon's got the Manchesters patrolling every town and street to keep the rumblings from becoming open rebellion. Their presence will only be seen as British aggression and sooner or later it will be met with rocks and stones and worse. And it's the rank and file that will bear the brunt. Boys like Jack's son, Peter.

ROBERT   I see. Has Jack heard anything from Peter?

NED   Oh, yes, a flimsy last week. "Having a smashing time in old Baghdad. Don't worry Da, we'll be home soon."

ROBERT   Right.

NED   "Cpl. Peter Dawkins, 2nd Manchesters, D Company, 3rd Platoon." King and Country, all that sort of rot.

ROBERT   If they only knew the truth.

NED   Do you think it would make any difference?

ROBERT   If we're hanging on to Arabia so Curzon can maintain control of India?…

NED   It's not the only reason.

ROBERT   There are others?

NED Oh yes. It bubbles up through the sand like oasis water. The Bedouin have no idea what to do with it because they can't drink it and since the British Navy is changing over from coal to oil—

ROBERT begins to cough and shake again.

ROBERT My God. We need a navy to keep our empire and we need an empire to keep our navy.

NED Now you've got it. Would you like to ring the bell for a while?

ROBERT Has it done you any good?

NED Not really, no.

ROBERT Then why don't you come out of there and do something about it?

NED Like what?

ROBERT Come out of that windowsill and be Lawrence of Arabia.

NED I don't want to be him anymore.

ROBERT A man that fights unselfishly for what he knows to be right?

NED Unselfishly? It's all I've ever tried to do, to do something perfect, without one trace of me in it. Some perfect gesture, some perfect accomplishment that doesn't reflect my own awful face back at me; but everything I do is poisoned by this cancer of "self" and I'm sick of it.

ROBERT What does that leave then, a prison sentence here in this little room?

NED Yes, neither effected nor effecting. Neither infected nor infectious.

ROBERT And that's why you're perched on a windowsill shouting that the world is full of cheats and liars? You can't stop caring, can you?

NED I don't want to care anymore, don't you see! I'm afraid, Robert, deathly afraid.

ROBERT Afraid you'll be hurt?

NED When we had wounded in the desert, those that were too badly injured to ride, we had to execute them ourselves so the Turks wouldn't torture them to death. When my boy Farraj was wounded, he was so young and fair, no one wanted to do it. So it fell to me. It was possibly the greatest and most perfect act of unselfish mercy, an act of pure love, that war has ever called into being and it was offered to me. But, when I took up the pistol, this pistol, and pointed it at his temple, there was a whisper in my soul "look at 'me' the caring, look at 'me' the merciful, look at 'me' the loving" and I shot him. For love of me.

ROBERT Haven't you perhaps suffered enough for that?

NED Not nearly enough.

ROBERT What would it take to show you you've suffered enough? A sign from God perhaps?

NED Wouldn't Oxford be lovely all covered in green grasshoppers? Or the Thames flowing red with blood? I'd settle for that. Or someone to take away all the firstborn.

ROBERT Did you miss it in the desert? In the mud, the firstborn were dropping like flies. Even some of the second and thirdborn. How could you not have noticed? They smell awfully after a few days. What more evidence do you want than the stench of bloated, rotting man, for the need for love?

NED Robert, the massacre of the firstborn isn't a sign from God. That's just man doing his very best.

ROBERT You can be very ugly sometimes.

NED All the world's great men are just frightened little shadows who struggle to prove themselves at the expense of all the marrying men and mothers of the world. We'd all be a lot better off if we all kept our pathetic little selves to ourselves. Go home to your wife and children. I thank you for your company, but please, please leave me alone.

ROBERT No.

NED No?

ROBERT No. I understand what you feel you must do. But that sentence is not my sentence. You don't want to care anymore. Fine. But you can't stop us from caring. Neither can you stop our love or admiration. You are loved. You are admired. And there is nothing you can do about it. You are sincerely loved and admired.

NED Please stop saying that. You're making me feel loved and admired.

ROBERT You're a genius, Lawrence. So says Feisal. So says Churchill. So says George Bernard Shaw. So say thousands of Arabs. So say I. And here you are ringing a bell in your underpants?

NED Be careful, Robert, I only truly admire those who don't fall for my tricks.

ROBERT I know.

NED And you're very close to being immune to them.

ROBERT Isn't it frightening?

NED I can't write my book. That bloody great bastard of a typewriter will not listen to a word I say.

ROBERT Then free yourself of it. What is it but the penance that the politicians and generals are so very glad you've sentenced yourself to? Seven years to write every mile you fought over, every bloody thorn, every stone, every expanse of desert?

NED Seven years re-killing all the dead.

ROBERT Seven years punishing yourself for being Lawrence of Arabia. I say come out of there and be Lawrence of Arabia. You want to wake the place up? Don't do it like this. Do it your way. Don't prove your love with a book. Prove your love with a bullet.

JACK comes in with tea.

JACK   Your tea, sirs.

ROBERT   I say there's not nearly enough shooting going on.

NED   Oh? And whom would you like me to shoot first?

> *ROBERT indicates NED's typewriter.*

ROBERT   That bloody great bastard for a start, who won't listen to a single word you say.

JACK   But sir—

ROBERT   It's all right, Jack, it's loaded with blanks. It's a symbolic execution.

> *NED thinks about it and then comes down from the window sill. He sets the bell down, looks at his gun, then points it at the typewriter.*

NED   Cover your ears, everyone, this is going to be loud.

> *JACK and ROBERT cover their ears and NED shoots the typewriter. It flies off the table in pieces as a bullet strikes it. The gun was loaded with live rounds after all.*

Good God, I seem to have executed my Royal Number Five.

JACK   Blanks, sir?

ROBERT   No, that was definitely a bullet.

NED   The shot heard round the world.

ROBERT   Or at least this room.

NED   That's the spirit. Jack, you're my adjutant. And since Robert is already a captain there's no sense demoting him. You're the captain. And we, the Oxford Roof Climbers, have had enough.

> *NED and ROBERT sit at tea to plot.*

JACK   Is there anything else I can do for you gentlemen? Toasted scone perhaps?

NED   Spoilsport. Fine, two scones then. Three if you haven't had breakfast.

JACK   Would you like some clotted cream, sirs?

NED & ROBERT   *(NED)* Mm, cream. *(ROBERT)* Oh, yes please.

> *The lads busy themselves with plotting over tea.*

••IV••

> *Lord CURZON's office, morning. NED and ROBERT sit as if they were students called before the headmaster. A wall clock ticks slowly.*

ROBERT   Do you think he's heard about the Roof Climbers' Rebellion?

NED   I'm sure he's heard about the Roof Climbers' Rebellion.

ROBERT   Isn't it wonderful?

NED   Oh, yes.

ROBERT   What do we do now?

NED   You've never been called into the headmaster's office, have you?

ROBERT   I... well... no.

NED   Pathetic.

> *ROBERT goes back to waiting, then as an afterthought.*

ROBERT   Have you ever been called into the headmaster's office?

NED   Never in my life and I resent the insinuation.

> *CURZON enters in full stride. NED and ROBERT stand for his entrance and then sit.*

CURZON   Gentlemen. I have here a report that states to the effect that sometime last night a party of persons...

NED   I beg your pardon, sir, but how many persons exactly does it say?

CURZON   A party.

NED   I see, that many? Sorry to interrupt. A party.

CURZON   Of persons unknown stole into the Magdelen College Grove and proceeded to kidnap the entire herd of College deer and drive them through the alleys of Oxford…

NED   Oh, deer!

> *ROBERT stifles a laugh.*

CURZON   Where, this morning, they were found to be quartered in the All Soul's Quadrangle. Well? What do you have to say for yourselves? Nothing. Then let's hear it from the deer then, shall we?

> *CURZON withdraws a letter, which he proceeds to read from.*

"Deerest Lord Curzon,
Before you came and declared the fields and trees of Oxford your own all of this was ours. Since then we have lived peacefully within your walls and boundaries but we must inform you that the situation is now untenable. Our rights as deer must be recognized. We have laid claim to the All Soul's Quad as an act of peaceful protest. In the spirit of brotherhood, we invite you to remain here as our guests, however, in compensation we think it only appropriate that you hand over to us all your sugar cubes."

> *CURZON hands the letter to NED.*

Quite an elaborate operation requiring quite a lot of coordination.

NED   Indeed, and how did they manage to hold the pen in their little hooves?

CURZON   Perhaps someone held the pen for them.

NED   No, that's their hoof writing all right. Dreadful scrawl.

> *NED returns the letter to CURZON.*

CURZON   It has also come to my attention that someone rang a bell in the All Soul's Quad last week waking several of the Fellows and that shortly thereafter there was heard a bang.

A rather loud bang. Not unlike a gunshot. This, gentlemen, is quite serious.

NED   An accidental discharge is quite serious. I believe Robert could help you in that regard. Robert?

ROBERT   Well, I believe... well, I believe that... we'd dropped a book. It was a large book.

NED & ROBERT   *(NED)* The Oxford English Dictionary *(ROBERT)* Melville's *Moby Dick*.

CURZON   Which?

NED   A rather large book. Dropped from rather high up.

CURZON   I am not without a sense of humour but somehow I believe this to be some other sort of thing.

NED   What other thing do you have in mind?

CURZON   Sabotage? Isn't that what you are an expert in? Blowing up the unsuspecting on trains? The sabotage of bridges, rails, et cetera?

NED   Et cetera, especially, made such a lovely show when it went up. But my Lord Curzon, the peace has been decided and I'm glad to say my sabotaging days are over, especially, the sabotaging of et cetera. Et cetera and I are great friends now, veritably chummy.

CURZON slams his hand on his desk.

CURZON   Do you mean by these little pranks to bring your Arab Revolt to Oxford?

NED   Perhaps, Lord Curzon, the Arab Revolt is already here. I need not remind you of the delicate state of things in the Empire. The women who worked the land and factories are hungry for the right to vote.

NED slams his hand down on the arm of his chair.

The Tommies back from the trenches with Karl Marx in their pockets.

NED slams his hand again.

What is it that you're afraid of, Vice Chancellor? That they might rise up and demand what was promised them?

> *NED slams his hand a third time.*

CURZON   What was promised them was peace, and peace is what they have, by God.

NED   They want more and they shall get it.

CURZON   What is it that they want? Let's ask one of the Tommies, fresh from the trenches then. Mr. Graves, if I'm not mistaken you were in the thick of it at the Battle of the Somme?

NED   Shrapnel through the lung. Finger. Thigh. Finger. Finger. Forehead.

ROBERT   Not as thick as some, sir.

CURZON   And now, how are your studies progressing at St. John's? English and Classics?

ROBERT   Terrible.

CURZON   And your shop, how is business?

ROBERT   Terrible.

CURZON   What about your young wife and children then? How are they?

ROBERT   …

CURZON   You see, Lawrence, given the choice, Mr. Graves here just wants things to be quiet. And I believe you'll be hard pressed to find any that want anything but. You try to move men like him and they'll show you what they want, the weekend, pudding at Christmas, every now and then a show. Children. You're mistaken if you think he wants anything else. Gravely mistaken.

> *Silence as CURZON peruses the file while the clock ticks. He finally closes the file.*

I don't think there is any more that needs to be said about the matter.

NED There is one more thing, Lord Curzon, I really must ask
you the time.

CURZON The time?

NED Yes. Of the day?

> *CURZON scrutinizes NED closely for several moments
> but NED betrays no ulterior motive. He sits quietly,
> almost innocently, waiting for someone to tell him the
> time. Lord CURZON carefully checks his watch... in
> a manner that is not unlike a man dealing with a time
> bomb.*

CURZON Ten o'clock in the morning.

NED Sharp?

CURZON A minute to. Do you have somewhere else to be?

NED Nowhere especially.

CURZON Very well then... Mr. Graves, I'd like to extend to you
the offer I made Lawrence some weeks ago. I think you
would be an ideal speaker at the upcoming memorial
service.

ROBERT For the glorious dead?

CURZON In honour of those who laid down their lives.

> *Pause*

No need to answer definitively just yet. There's still time. Do
think about it. I think it might be just the thing for you.

> *ROBERT looks to NED.*

Don't look to him for answers. Lawrence isn't quite as retired
from Middle Eastern affairs as he seems. Since he was
veritably dismissed from the Paris peace talks last year he
has simply shifted his attention to secret correspondences
and anonymous letters to the press championing Feisal's
demands. Actions which have directly heightened tensions in
Syria. The French have already suffered casualties over the
matter. Lawrence's retirement may yet prove more deadly
than his career. I should think, Mr. Graves, the best course of

action would be to leave Lawrence to his sedition and concentrate your energies on putting the war behind you.

ROBERT   And how in the name of God do you suppose I do that?

CURZON   I leave that, Mr. Graves, up to you.

> *The clock chimes ten bells. There is a knock at the door. They sit in silence. Again there is a knock.*

Yes?

JACK   *(off)* A delivery, your Lordship.

CURZON   Who are you? A delivery? From whom?

JACK   *(off)* Doesn't say, my Lord. Looks quite official and if you don't mind me saying, sir, heavy like affairs of state.

CURZON   How did you get in here?

JACK   *(off)* Your secretary sent me up, sir. Told me to bring this right in.

NED   Your Lordship, if this is an inconvenient time, Captain Graves and I could excuse ourselves and come back at a later date, say like, a week from never?

CURZON   No, Lawrence, I'm not finished with you yet.

JACK   *(off)* I'll deliver it later, sir.

CURZON   No, bring it in, man, and get out.

> *Without a glance at ROBERT or NED, JACK enters with a huge mounted rack of deer horns. He deposits the horns on Lord CURZON's desk and just as quickly exits.*

NED   It seems to me the deer have chosen their sovereign Lord. Since you never managed to become PM, I think this might just be your chance to retire from politics and go be King instead.

> *CURZON rises, takes up his hat and cane.*

CURZON   I see. If you'll excuse me gentlemen, I've forgotten an appointment. Some chums from the Foreign Office have invited me hunting and I'm an excellent shot.

CURZON exits.

NED   Well, Robert, what do you think of that? Not a bad parting shot, but he did yield to us the field. Shall we rearrange the furniture to celebrate?

> *NED jumps up and moves some of the office furniture. He removes one of CURZON's portraits and hangs the deer horns.*

ROBERT   I'm late for tutorial.

NED   Don't go yet, let's go down to Fuller's. We'll clap for service – that gets them every time.

ROBERT   Does it? Does it cause a scene?

NED   Why so glum? We've won, don't you see?

ROBERT   We haven't won. He's right about everything.

NED   Oh, don't mind what he said about your family. He was just trying to get your goat... or should I say get your deer?

ROBERT   Curzon's right. I'm the biggest hypocrite of them all. A wife and babies, a shop for God's sake. That man will be working on his memoirs and in the grave, and there will still be men dying in the mess he created.

NED   A man can choose to be whatever sort of man he likes.

ROBERT   I'm sorry, but he can't.

> *ROBERT coughs.*

I have to go back to them. I'm no warrior. You are. I'll go back to my family and since you aren't all that blocked, you can go back to writing your secret correspondences and anonymous letters to the press.

NED   I haven't written a damn thing but that letter of protest from the deer.

ROBERT   I have to go home to Nancy and the children. Even if it…

NED   Even if it what? Kills you? A long and lingering death trying to hide your cough from them? You think you can spare Nancy the pain but you can't. You and Nancy will simply go on pretending nothing's wrong until one day, you no longer recognize each other's faces. But I do understand, what kind of man would you be if you turned and ran away from love?

ROBERT   A man like you.

NED   You don't want to be that. Trust me. Go home.

>   *ROBERT moves to go.*

I'll just have to hang these trousers from the pinnacle of Radcliffe Camera by myself.

>   *NED unfurls a pair of black trousers from his satchel and holds them in front of himself as if he's seeing how they fit.*

I bribed Curzon's tailor. Cost me three quid but I think it was worth it.

ROBERT   To fly from the top of Radcliffe Camera?

NED   The impossible climb.

ROBERT   Impossible.

NED   That's what they say. The ascent of Mount Sinai, Everest, heaven. Radcliffe Camera.

>   *ROBERT can see the Radcliffe Camera from the window. He turns back to NED.*

ROBERT   The sides look easy enough.

NED   It's the dome. No hand holds for forty feet.

ROBERT   It's awfully dangerous.

NED   It's your favourite kind.

ROBERT You know, Ned, I think you might just be the most dangerous man alive.

NED I know. Isn't it frightening?

> *NED tosses the trousers at ROBERT who can do nothing but catch them.*

••V••

> *The Graves' shop, a kind of small grocer and teashop.*
> *NANCY hurries to open for business. She pulls the*
> *cashbox from its hiding spot and goes to count it, but*
> *doesn't. She ties an apron around her back while moving*
> *to open the door and Lord CURZON steps in,*
> *a newspaper under his arm. NANCY is startled.*

CURZON My apologies. I didn't mean to startle you.

NANCY No, I'm sorry. I was in a rush. Good heavens.

CURZON Good heavens. You are open for business? I may return at a more convenient time.

NANCY No, no, please, do come in. I was just going to have cup of tea. Would you care for some?

CURZON Yes, I do think I will. You're most kind.

NANCY Well, you're most welcome.

> *NANCY goes about preparing some cups of tea.*
> *CURZON looks about the shop.*

CURZON So this is the poet's shop of poet's hill?

NANCY We have developed a reputation as that but we do have other clientele.

CURZON Have you met anyone famous?

NANCY Well, the poet laureate, Robert Bridges, does drop by from time to time. And the Masefields… who else? Let's see—

CURZON I would like to speak to the proprietor, Captain Graves.

NANCY My husband isn't in, sir.

CURZON I beg your pardon, Mrs. Graves.

NANCY Miss Nicholson, Mr. Graves' wife.

CURZON I do apologize, I thought you were the help.

NANCY Your tea, sir.

CURZON Ah yes. Lovely. Nothing like a spot of tea after a bit of morning cycling. That hill was quite something.

NANCY It's a lot more fun on the way down. You'll have to do without sugar, I'm afraid.

CURZON I understood your husband minded the shop on Tuesdays.

NANCY He's sleeping, the poor thing.

CURZON Who is looking after the children?

NANCY The nanny.

CURZON The nanny. How very nice. Business must be brisk. Out late last night?

NANCY …

CURZON Mr. Graves, the poor thing?

NANCY He looked after our daughter last night, who has a bit of a cough, so that I could open up this morning.

CURZON Very nice of him.

NANCY Is there anything I can help you with, Lord Curzon?

CURZON Has Lawrence of Arabia come round?

NANCY He has been by the shop. He dropped by last week.

CURZON What was your impression of the man?

NANCY My husband was minding the shop that day. He bought our complete inventory of sugar cubes.

CURZON   So you haven't actually met Lawrence personally?

NANCY   I haven't had the honour, yet, no.

CURZON   I see, I see. Then this is a matter between Mr. Graves and myself. I won't do him and yourself the discourtesy of troubling you with it.

NANCY   Mr. Graves and I are on equal terms and I don't mind the discourtesy.

CURZON   Very well. You are aware that your husband and Colonel Lawrence have been spending a considerable lot of time together?

NANCY   They've been spending some time together, yes.

CURZON   And I'm sure you've heard of the recent rash of hooliganism that has plagued several of the colleges?

> *CURZON unfolds his newspaper.*

Yesterday's *Oxonian*. "Large Trousers Flown from Pinnacle of Radcliffe Camera." And they've printed a photograph.

NANCY   Oh, and I see there was a bit of a breeze.

CURZON   "What life to lead and where to go after the war, after the war? Questions on many an ex soldier's lips, young and old, officers and men; is home truly played out? Is there something that can be done for England, to free it from all the English stay-at-homes? And how does one identify these cads and touts? Look close, Oxford, stand watch, Manchester, London, Dover. You can spot the traitor if you keep a sharp and vigilant eye. He'll be the one calling for more troops in cabinet clad only in his underpants. Dib, dib, dob. The Oxford Roof Climbers' Rebellion." What life to lead and where to go after the war, after the war? Cad and tout?

> *CURZON presents a copy of ROBERT's book* Over the Brazier.

That sounds like something your husband wrote? Encouraging, and I daresay leading, rebellious behaviour could be interpreted as downright bolshie.

NANCY   Bolshie? A bit of undergraduate fun, I should think.

CURZON   Need I remind you, Miss Graves – Nicholson, that victory has not brought about a peace which is business as usual. People have killed and been killed and there are many survivors with unanswered questions; why did we kill, why did we die and why was I spared? Now, what if someone were to promise to answer this question: a person that seems to be able to make dreams reality, answer hopes and heal pain?

NANCY   Is it the second coming already? I thought it was just now half-past eight?

CURZON   We have today received a document, a manifesto, if you will, from the very Oxford Roof Climbers' Rebellion.

> *He produces a booklet of paper, bound with some lengths of black bootlace. It looks like a ten-page essay handed in for grading.*

The situation is now critical and strict disciplinary measures are being considered. Any members that are not fully committed to such an organization should distance themselves from it immediately.

NANCY   Lord Curzon, I can assure you that my husband had nothing to do with that article, there are some clumsy references to one of his poems, but that could have been written by any undergraduate or aspiring soldier poet familiar with his work. Your concerns are unfounded and, if I may say so, sir, silly. My husband's friendship with Lawrence is literary. He helps Robert with his poems and Robert returns the favour by helping him write his book.

CURZON   Thomas Edward Lawrence is a little Emperor, and people, people like your husband, are his army. Lawrence walks away from the battle, his armies do not and to belabour the analogy, the war is never won.

NANCY   That may or may not be so, but it is absolutely not for me, or you, to say how much time my husband spends with his friends.

CURZON   How many of your husband's friends does he spend the night with on a regular basis?

NANCY   …

CURZON   Such relations, in some circles, may seem to be a bit… how should I say this? Unnatural.

NANCY   Is this what you've come for? To slander and scandalize?

CURZON   I came to speak to your husband.

NANCY   Well, as you can see he isn't here, so unless there is something I can help you find? Some sugar perhaps?

CURZON   No, thank you, but should I need any I'll send for some.

> *CURZON holds his empty cup of tea out to NANCY. After a pause, NANCY comes to take it.*

NANCY   If I'm not mistaken, Lord Curzon, you are the President and Founder of the Anti-Suffrage League?

CURZON   Yes, as a matter of fact I am.

NANCY   It won't be long now and we'll have the vote, you know?

CURZON   Actually, I'm beginning to soften on that question.

NANCY   Really?

CURZON   I believe the right to vote is wasted on most everyone, why should women be excluded? I do hope you pass on my greetings to Mr. Nicholson.

NANCY   Mr. Nicholson is my father.

CURZON   Oh yes, of course. My mistake. Matters of this kind are so confusing in this day and age. Mr. Graves is your husband. Mr. Nicholson is your father and, of course, your brother. Unless your father was one of those unfortunate men whose wife bore him no sons.

NANCY   My mother bore my father a son. He was killed in France. Good day, sir… please… if you would be so kind as to leave the premises. Your long ride downhill is waiting.

ROBERT   *(off)* Nancy, I thought it was my day today.

> *ROBERT enters, in a rush, wearing the clothes he was wearing from the day before.*

CURZON   Mister Graves.

ROBERT   Lord Curzon.

CURZON   I do hope your daughter's cough is no longer troubling her.

ROBERT   No, it's fine. Is there something I can do for you, Lord Curzon?

CURZON   Your wife has been more than helpful.

ROBERT   You came to call on my wife?

NANCY   His lordship came to speak to you, Robert.

ROBERT   Really? What about?

CURZON   Whether or not you had given any thought to the request I made of you?

NANCY   What request?

CURZON   Whether Captain Graves would speak at a memorial service in honour of the lost of the Great War.

ROBERT   …

NANCY   I don't think that we would at all be interested.

CURZON   Do ask the man of the house if he's had a chance to rethink his position.

> *With that, Lord CURZON exits. NANCY and ROBERT stand in silence. Then ROBERT moves to go about to open the shop. He gestures to NANCY's apron.*

ROBERT   Is that my apron?

NANCY   Yours is in…

> *ROBERT steps out of the room to fetch his apron. NANCY takes up the manifesto and reads it to herself. Straightaway the emotions she has been suppressing come and threaten to overwhelm her.*

NANCY   I will not... I am better than... I am stronger than... don't you dare. No, no. No.

> *She shakes as if a flood of grief and anger is going to burst forth but she masters it. ROBERT re-enters tying his apron behind him.*

ROBERT   I honestly did think it was my day today.

NANCY   It was your day today but my husband was not in my bed when I awoke this morning. Oh, don't worry about the children, they're with Mrs. Masefield. Where were you last night? Think quickly, Robert.

ROBERT   I'm sorry, Ned and I were writing last night and we got a little carried away.

NANCY   Well, that's good then. You were with Ned, getting carried away. How's his book coming?

ROBERT   It's coming along just fine.

NANCY   And yours?

ROBERT   ...

NANCY   All those late nights and tonight, until well past dawn? Writing the night away, you must have pages and pages of the stuff, just piling up and ready for the printers? Where is it then?

ROBERT   I left it with Ned. For proofing.

NANCY   Well, how about another eye then? Bring forth the verses. I've got some time since no one ever comes into this shop. Since we are on the verge of bankruptcy I could look at some drafts.

ROBERT   ...

NANCY   I see. No verses, no book. No book, no money, Robert. You can't write, can you? You can't write.

ROBERT   I told you, I left it with Ned.

NANCY   Do you want to know what I think? I don't think you and Ned do any writing at all. I think you and Ned… I think Ned has you.

ROBERT   That's ridiculous.

NANCY   Is it? Look into my eyes and tell me it isn't true. He has you, doesn't he?

ROBERT   He doesn't.

NANCY   Then who does? Poetry? Me? I don't have you.

ROBERT   I love you, Nancy, I do.

NANCY   So what pulls you away, Robert?

ROBERT   Nobody has me but dead men have me. They with heads riddled with bullet holes have me. They walk out of the grocers carrying sacks for old ladies. In the library, men with no lower jaws bring stacks of books up to share a table with me. Eyeless men, late to lecture, ring their bicycle bells as they pass me on Cornmarket…

NANCY   We're not talking about the war.

ROBERT   It's exactly what we're talking about. When I lie beside you at night—

NANCY   I don't want to talk about the war—

ROBERT   Oh, yes, you don't want it in your house. Well, it's already in your house. When I lie beside you at night shells come in and land on our bed and smash us limbless into the trees. I'm a dead man, don't you see? I'm dead but I still go on walking and talking. And the dead are everywhere, trying to tell me that I can no longer go on playing house.

NANCY   Is that what we're doing? Playing house? Haven't I done everything to bring you back from the dead?

ROBERT   You have. Everything. But there's something still that is missing. And I don't know what it is.

NANCY   You know exactly what it is.

ROBERT   What's that?

> *NANCY holds out the manifesto to ROBERT.*

NANCY   A bit of undergraduate fun. Go on, read it.

ROBERT   "We the undersigned do declare, in memory of the glorious dead, one thousand days of mourning for humanity, curled in a ball and mute for shame. All those who do not immediately comply will be shot, upon which time, one thousand days of mourning will promptly begin. All those who do not immediately comply will be shot, upon which time..."

> *ROBERT turns the pages and sees that the manifesto repeats this chain ad infinitum.*

"Forever and ever, amen. The Oxford Roof Climbers' Rebellion." Nancy, I never wrote this.

NANCY   Is that what's missing, a thousand days of mourning for humanity? Or the shooting of all those who don't immediately comply? It sounds so very easy but whom do we shoot first? Oh, yes, the first one who doesn't curl into a ball, mute for shame. Who will that be? Me? Jenny? David? I am not ashamed I survived.

ROBERT   But I am, don't you see? Everyone else was killed. I am ashamed I survived. I'm sick with shame.

NANCY   Then what do we do to cure you of it?

ROBERT   I don't know.

NANCY   Then what?

ROBERT   I don't know.

NANCY   Then we go on, slowly, imperceptibly towards the freedom we want to live. You write it, I draw it, we plant it, we build it.

ROBERT   Oh God!

NANCY   What? You don't believe in it. Look at me. You don't think we can do it, do you?

ROBERT   No, not like this.

NANCY   Would you truly kill to be free of it?

> *ROBERT begins to cough and shake.*

You never wrote it but you may as well have. I'm going home. You mind the shop. It's your day.

> *NANCY moves to exit.*

Oh, Lord Curzon wanted his trousers. He thought you might know their whereabouts.

> *ROBERT is shaking violently and can't catch his breath.*

Robert? Robert, what's the matter?

> *ROBERT's eyes roll back in his head as he collapses. NANCY dashes between ROBERT and the possible remedies.*

Robert, raise your head and—let me run and get—let me fetch you some—

> *As quickly as NANCY can think of something that might help, just as quickly she knows it won't.*

Oh my God, I don't know what to do, tell me what to do?

> *She falls to her knees beside him waiting for an answer from ROBERT who cannot speak a word.*

Oh my God, Robert… oh my God…

> *NANCY is however, the only witness to ROBERT's suffering.*

••VI••

> *Late night, NED's rooms. NED sits in a chair with his head in hands. There is a knock at the door. NED collects up a handful of telegrams. He tidies up the newspapers from several continents, hiding their headlines. He looks at his hands, and realizes they are*

> *black with newsprint. He pours some water in a small basin to wash the ink from his hands.*

NED Come in, Jack, it's open.

> *ROBERT enters, NED's gift of Arab robes folded under his arm.*

Robert. I wasn't expecting you. Would you care for some tea?

ROBERT No.

NED Well, then it's a good thing because I haven't got any.

ROBERT You were expecting Jack?

NED It's nearly four in the morning, but plenty of time for mischief yet. Have a seat and let's plot shall we?

ROBERT I won't be that long.

NED Dissension in the ranks? Come now, tell me what's wrong. Permission to speak freely. On your way here just now, did you notice a small red flag flying from the pinnacle of All Soul's—

ROBERT …

NED A small red flag? It sounds to me like the flag of the Hejaz. The Holy Land. Mecca.

ROBERT How did it get up there?

> *ROBERT places the robes on NED's table.*

NED I can't imagine. It must have been a daring climb though.

ROBERT You can't make England Arabia.

NED Neither can we make Arabia England.

> *ROBERT presents the manifesto. NED dries his hands with a towel.*

ROBERT "We the undersigned do declare, in memory of the glorious dead, one thousand days of mourning for humanity, curled in a ball and mute for shame. All those who do not immediately comply will be shot, upon which time, one thousand days of mourning will promptly begin." Would you like me to read on? There's pages and pages of it. "All those who do not immediately comply will be shot, upon which time." "Immediately comply will be shot." "Will be shot." My wife thinks I wrote this.

NED   You can tell Nancy I wrote it.

ROBERT   This is not what I wanted.

NED   Oh, and what did you want?

ROBERT   I wanted something that would make a difference.

NED   That will make a difference.

ROBERT   Not this. This is neverending suffering. Nihilistic remembrance.

NED   We're sentenced to neverending remembrance, why shouldn't they be?

ROBERT   But this is not humanly possible.

NED   Exactly, my friend, exactly. Humans are weak. They hunger and they whinge for food. When they're thirsty, they refuse to march. Sleepy, they fold up their legs and lie down. When angry they bash at skulls. They lust and they letch inside each other and they are never ever satisfied. I don't want humanity. I want more.

ROBERT   It isn't possible.

NED   It is possible. They can be better than themselves. They just have to be—

ROBERT   More like you?

NED   They just have to be afraid. I am not a military genius. I know one single truth about all living things that makes me powerful. You remember how we led the deer from Magdalen College into the All Soul's quad?

ROBERT   Yes, Jack and I led them with handfuls of sugar cubes.

NED   And I followed behind with a switch. Animals and humans concern themselves with two things, what they desire and what they fear. Of the two, fear is stronger by a nose. All you've got to do is offer them what they desire and remind them what they're afraid of and they'll go absolutely anywhere you want them to go.

ROBERT   And this is where you want them to go? Into a room like this, to do nothing but dwell on the past, to curl in a ball and brood over the wrongs that have been done to them? Out there, Ned, is God, people working with their hands, people who try to love in spite of their fears. In spite of men like you. Your way is wrong, fear and want are not the only things that move people.

NED   You don't know a damn thing do you?

> *NED takes his shirt off and is just wearing a wrinkled white singlet. NED turns and pulls up his singlet to display his back to ROBERT.*

ROBERT   My God, your back...

> *ROBERT approaches, coming closer to NED, reaching out but not touching.*

How did you get those?

NED   I was captured in the war. The price on my head was twenty thousand pounds but they had no idea it was me. It didn't make a difference because they were after something other than money. I resisted and they whipped me into submission. That was only the beginning...

ROBERT   You were...

NED   It was the only time and it was that. So there was part of me that enjoyed it. I enjoyed it, don't you see? God granted me a glimpse of how pathetic we really are. You want wisdom? We are little flesh vessels and all we do is want. Do you even know why you had children? Have you done anything but curse two more people, trapped them in a prison of skin and bone, to allay your own little selfish desires and fears? You want something that makes a difference, Robert? The truth is, that absolutely nothing makes a difference. We desire and fear and we desire and fear and then we're dead.

ROBERT   There is one other thing – stronger than those two.

NED   I know what you are going to say.

ROBERT   Love.

NED   That, soldier, is the most dangerous want of all and should be feared the most.

ROBERT   Love is the absolute and only way. You could be its perfect example. You're just afraid to try.

NED   Should this be allowed to love? Could this possibly be loved?

> *ROBERT goes to touch NED's scars.*

Don't you dare, now get out.

> *Just then there is a knock at the door. The both of them pause and look at the door but neither of them, especially NED, moves to answer it. ROBERT looks at NED and sees fear on his face. NED walks to the door, takes a breath and reaches to open it. He swings the door open. NED seems relieved to find it is Lord CURZON at the door.*

It seems we aren't the only ones in Oxford not sleeping tonight. Please, Lord Curzon, do come in and join us. I was just telling Robert a funny story.

CURZON   Mr. Graves.

ROBERT   Lord Curzon.

NED   Now, where was I?

CURZON   Lawrence, I really don't care for…

NED   Well, I do. I do care for.

CURZON   Enough. You've read the papers?

NED   Today? Or the last few months? I do have them here. Would you like to take some clippings for your scrapbook?

CURZON   No more games now, you've heard from Feisal. I know you have been corresponding. Pulling the strings behind my back. Captain Graves, did you know that at the Paris peace talks Lawrence often acted as translator for Prince Feisal, a man who can speak perfect French and English? And that when Lawrence was translating Feisal's Arabic, Feisal was simply reciting passages of the *Koran*, and Lawrence was dictating Arab demands himself?

ROBERT   I did not, but it sounds just like him.

CURZON   You're beginning to understand him. He's made a dramatic show of retirement and then manipulates everything from there; dangerous machinations that have led directly to this uprising.

NED   The Oxford Roof Climbers' Rebellion?

CURZON   Lawrence. The rebellion in Mesopotamia. A British outpost has been overrun in Mosul. A Shiite jihad has been declared in Karbala. Insurgents are laying siege to the towns of Samawa and Rumaitha.

NED   And we're putting the uprising down with everything we have, does that about sum it up?

CURZON   Feisal must have informed you about the column of Manchesters wiped out yesterday in a village of goat herds?

NED   Hillah. A lovely bit of fun that must have been.

> *NED moves to again wash his hands in the basin.*

CURZON   Lawrence, this is your fault—

NED   I'm not the cause of every bit of butchery in the world. Give the world some credit.

CURZON   Feisal is under your direct control, isn't he?

> *NED dries his hands.*

NED   Feisal and his family are in exile in Italy. The French are fighting for control of Syria. And there is no control in Mesopotamia.

CURZON   You've got blood on your hands, Lawrence.

> *NED throws his towel at CURZON.*

NED If I've got blood on my hands then so do you.

CURZON I'm doing my best for the bloody place.

NED Like the best you did for India?

CURZON Exactly.

NED A boy learns to tie his shoes. He cannot quite get it. His mother swats his hands away and ties them for him. Now, he has a well-tied pair of shoes, but the glare at his mother is quite unmistakable. Sound familiar?

CURZON I wonder what your Arab friends would think of such an analogy.

NED I will endeavour to make no analogies in the future.

CURZON I'm here to ask you… to demand—

NED You're not in any position to make demands.

CURZON I'm the British Foreign Secretary and you are merely Colonel Lawrence.

NED Merely? I am Lawrence of Arabia, El Aurens, the Uncrowned King of Damascus, the White Prince of the Desert.

CURZON I demand you take down that flag. British soldiers are dead and you are flying a flag of the enemy over their mothers.

NED I will not remove the flag.

CURZON You are a traitor, a traitor to the Crown, a traitor to your home.

NED I will not take down the flag until we give up Arabia and you retire, Lord Curzon. Those are my demands.

CURZON It is my duty to inform you sir, that your demands are punishable by death.

ROBERT Ned.

CURZON By death.

NED Then so be it.

l to r: Paul Rainville, Victor Ertmanis, Tom Rooney.
Photo by Cylla von Tiedemann.

> *JACK enters.*

ROBERT Jack.

NED Come in, Jack. We're having a little tea party, if you've brought any.

JACK I didn't bring any tea.

NED Do come in anyway. Have you got mischief on your mind?

CURZON Lawrence, I'd like to see you in my office this morning at ten o'clock. I'll let myself out.

JACK You're not going anywhere.

CURZON What in God's name is wrong with you, man?

> *JACK crosses, draws open NED's table drawer, and withdraws NED's revolver.*

NED Do please sit down, Lord Curzon.

CURZON sits.

JACK   Since my boy learned to walk he went marching about the room. Every stick he ever picked up became a rifle or a sabre. His heroes were always men like you sir, Alexander, Caesar, Wellington. So it was no surprise to me, and his mum, that he chose to serve his country as a soldier.

ROBERT   Why don't you give me that gun, Jack?

JACK   If it's all the same to you, sir, I'm going to hang on to it for a minute. It's time to put an end to all this.

ROBERT   And how do you propose we do that?

JACK   With shooting, sir, you said it yourself, there's not nearly enough shooting going on. There's been a lot of it over in the desert, it's only fair there was some shooting over here, don't you think? How about this bloody great bastard for a start? The one that won't listen to a single word you say? A symbolic execution?

ROBERT   I didn't mean this.

JACK   Oh, then what did you mean?

ROBERT   Just please give me the gun.

NED   Why, Robert? You called for firing squads. Here's a firing squad.

ROBERT   That's not what I meant.

NED   Oh, what did you mean? Cut all the Union Jacks into blindfolds, isn't that what you said?

ROBERT   I was speaking out of—

NED   Which? Fear or desire or love? What was your theory about bullets? No more bullets by the millions. One is all it'll take. It just has to be aimed in the right direction. Where did you say you wanted it pointed?

ROBERT   …

NED   Where? At bloody great bastards like Curzon.

ROBERT   I was wrong. I know now what I want.

NED   Oh, yes, love. You loved your son, didn't you Jack?

JACK   I loved him very much.

NED   But it didn't stop him from being killed did it?

JACK   No, it didn't. It didn't at all.

ROBERT   Give me the gun, Jack.

NED   Prove your love with a bullet.

JACK   I want the man to blame to pay for this.

ROBERT   Curzon's not to blame—

NED   I am.

> *JACK doesn't know who to point the gun at.*

I am. Do you want to know how I would destroy a column of Manchesters? I'd set an explosive in the road and detonate it under the first platoon. From buildings on both sides of the column would come heavy rifle and machine gun fire, with snipers targeting their leaders.

ROBERT   Lawrence, stop it. Jack—

NED   When they attempted a fighting withdrawal out the way they came, I would detonate my second explosive. That would break them into confused squads and sections trying desperately to regroup or carry out their wounded. But at every alley and window they would find more rifles.

ROBERT   Don't listen to him, Jack, he's using you—

NED   One last officer might organize what was left, try to hold a building until relief came but a good rush or two and they'd be overwhelmed.

JACK   That's how you would do it?

NED   Exactly.

ROBERT   Yes, Lawrence and then it would be all over.

NED   It would not be over one bit. The victors would strip and loot the bodies. The mob would come out with their sticks and torches, mutilate them, set them alight, string them up.

> *JACK points his gun at NED.*

ROBERT Put it down, Jack. Put it down. Someone has to be the first to do without this.

JACK Not me, don't ask it of me.

ROBERT I'm asking you Jack, don't do this. Don't honour him this way.

NED Young Peter dragged naked and dead by the laughing wogs through the streets of this Hillah.

> *JACK's gun lowers and his shoulders fall slightly. The danger is nearly past.*

JACK Oh, my poor wee baby boy.

ROBERT No!

> *Boom. JACK shoots NED. There is a line of grey smoke that streaks and hazes around NED's head. The smoke drifts and the echo rings through the room.*

NED I'm sorry, Jack, I'm sorry down to my empty soul.

JACK Well, good then. All this for your empty soul? It's careless of you. Awfully fecking careless, if you pardon me saying.

NED I do pardon you for saying. I do.

JACK Speak up you. Did you say something? Out with it?

NED …

JACK That's what I thought.

> *JACK gives ROBERT the pistol and walks out. ROBERT breaks the gun open on its latch and spills out the blank shells into his hand. ROBERT turns to NED.*

ROBERT Blanks. Why didn't you say something?

NED I did it to prove something to you. I did it for you, Robert.

ROBERT Did you really?

> *ROBERT puts the bullets on NED's table and exits with the revolver. NED pours CURZON a drink and hands it to him.*

CURZON Jack lost his son?

NED The column of Manchesters at Hillah, Peter was among them. I received a telegram from Churchill last night. Jack could have only just received word.

CURZON His commanding officer is to receive the Victoria Cross posthumously.

NED I'm sure his parents will be very proud. I'd appreciate it terribly if Jack was left alone. I don't think he's dangerous, merely heartbroken.

CURZON Are you going to lower your flag?

NED I will. I meant to suggest that all lands are holy but that isn't very true is it?

CURZON I've spent my entire life serving the Empire on which the sun never sets. Well, Lawrence, thanks to you and others like you, the sun is setting on us. You will have your way and we shall lose your Arabia to Baghdad and Damascus and Cairo and all the others that want their own country. And my India, we shall lose that too. Mark me, Lawrence, the sun will set on the British Empire, and my whole life will have been for what? You've no answer to that? What about this then? If the Indians are to have India and the Arabs are to have Arabia, what are the British to have?

NED For the life of me, I believe it was somewhere around here. Do you think there's any hope in finding it again?

CURZON I believe I shall not live so long.

> *CURZON moves for the door.*

NED Peace be upon you, your Lordship.

CURZON *Wah alaykum ah salaam, Lawrence.*

NED Call me Ned, if you like.

CURZON Thank you, I don't think I will.

CURZON exits. NED is left alone looking at the pile of bullets on the table. ROBERT walks out to speak at the church alone.

ROBERT   You may think your tragedy to be indelible. You may feel the things you saw burned into your memory forever. And like the newly minted monument outside this church you will feel that no one gazing upon it could ever forget. But it is as certain as the sunrise that your monuments too will gather pigeons and derelicts. Your glorious dead will be forgotten. Your heroes will be stale photographs. Your grief will just fill old graveyards. And out of all these things, the thing that will be most forgotten is why it happened. And war will happen again. You will say to me, "no, not this time, not this time. Never forget, we will never forget." And perhaps you won't. Perhaps even your children won't. But theirs will. Don't be angry with your grandchildren. People forget. It's how they remember how to survive. We forget the horror so we can carry on. The tragedy is this. There is wisdom to be found in war that is unfortunately forgotten with all the rest of the pain. The wisdom invisibly marked in the land by bones in farmer's fields. The wisdom whispered by arrowheads in riverbeds and musket balls buried deep in tree trunks. A war there is a war here. An enemy killed is an enemy created. Every pace you march into another man's home is one pace farther from your own. This is the thing to be remembered before you start the next one.

ROBERT humbly returns home.

••VII••

The Graves' cottage, morning. NANCY folds laundry.

NANCY   So you've done it.

ROBERT   As best I could.

NANCY   You had it your way.

ROBERT   I did.

NANCY   I'm sure the congregation was scandalized. You've won. Do you feel better now?

ROBERT   Not really.

NANCY   Then why did you do it?

ROBERT   There was a man killed in the war. I couldn't betray him.

NANCY   But you could betray us?

ROBERT   If that's what it took to lay him to rest, then so be it.

NANCY   And now you've laid him to rest, what are you going to do?

ROBERT   I don't know yet. But I am done at least. I'm done with it.

NANCY   Done.

ROBERT   The army, schools, religions, movements. Socialism. Any ism. The old England and the new one. I'm done with them too. I'm a poet. I cannot be rallied under any banner but the flag of procrastination.

NANCY   Do you think it's that easy?

ROBERT   I declare that I will belong to no organized body or institution from this day forth, so help me God.

NANCY   Oh, what about this institution? Us? Are you done with me?

ROBERT   I'm here, aren't I?

NANCY   Oh, yes, you're here, but where's my husband?

ROBERT   Here I am. Where are you?

NANCY   How dare you? I've been here, with the children, every single day. Do you think that's what I want to be, a nagging wife, counting pennies, bringing the bloody laundry off the line? Waiting dutifully for you to come home from the war?

ROBERT   Home is the war.

NANCY   Not here, not in this house.

ROBERT   Then perhaps I should leave.

NANCY   Then perhaps you should.

ROBERT   I'm going to look in on the children.

> *Silence.*

NANCY   The war is not you. The war is not me and the war is most certainly not my children.

ROBERT   Pretend all you want. It happened and it's us now. You haven't been keeping home, Nancy, you've been doing your very best to forget it.

> *ROBERT goes upstairs. NANCY pushes the laundry basket and laundry onto the floor. She then moves to exit out the door but finds NED standing there in travelling gear; tweed coat, hat and bag slung over his shoulder.*

NANCY   At long last, Mr. Lawrence.

NED   At long last, Miss Nicholson… is Robert home?

NANCY   Can Robert come out to play, is that what you mean?

NED   …

NANCY   He's upstairs, should I fetch him for you?

NED   No, please, I hate goodbyes.

NANCY   You're leaving.

NED   Is it that obvious?

NANCY   I should think it completely in character, you blowing things up and then running off without a scratch.

> *NANCY kneels to pick up the laundry.*

NED   I know what I've done here. I know what I've done to you.

NANCY   Do you?

NED   Yes.

l to r: Michelle Giroux, Tom Rooney.
Photo by Cylla von Tiedemann.

NANCY   Is that why you've popped by? You've had a twinge of guilt and now Lawrence of Arabia has come out of retirement to fix things for everyone?

NED   Luckily I don't have to fix everything, just the things I'm responsible for.

NANCY   Arabia?

NED   Arabia and other things.

   Silence.

NANCY   What is Robert to you?

NED   I have a confession to make. I can't make a straight answer. I am a parable maker, a storyteller, but within these bounds I always tell absolutely everything I know, to anyone who will listen. It annoys most everyone and those I am not interested in. I want only those who seek my answers, my truths, my wisdoms. Find my Holy Grail, so to speak. I have not repented my ways, after this I am going to go right back to making riddles so please, I beg of you, pay attention. I am in truth a mirror of a man. I am no one without someone to reflect. I used to reflect perfect things, desert moon rises, camel boys whose only possession was their loyalty to me, the smiles of my brothers Frank and Will... and so for a while I was perfect.

NANCY   You wanted to reflect Robert.

NED   Something, someone more perfect than myself.

NANCY   Why him? Why not your brothers?

NED   They were both killed in the war. We used to cycle to the Oxford School for Boys from our house over on Polstead, eldest first, youngest last.

NANCY   I had a brother killed in the war. We cycled together too. It was spring and the air made our hands chilly. He stopped us, leaned our bicycles against a fence, took my freezing hands in his and warmed them with his breath... I'd nearly forgotten that.

> *NED awkwardly, and by a great internal willpower, takes up both of NANCY's hands to comfort her. With any luck, this will be the first time anyone makes physical contact with NED.*

NED   I wouldn't forget, if I were you.

NANCY   You are a very, very clever man, Lawrence.

NED   So they say.

> *She smiles at him. He smiles back and lets her hands go. ROBERT comes in and stops at the door.*

There you are, Robert, I was just boring Nancy with a story about the great Bedu warrior, Auda Abu Tayi. We were dining in Prince Feisal's tent...

NANCY   I'll leave you two alone.

ROBERT   No, Nancy... please, stay, if you like. What do you want?

NED   My book.

ROBERT   I thought you were blocked?

NED   I was but I've just recently died and risen again unblocked.

> *NED takes a nearly inch-thick package out of his bag and holds it out to ROBERT. ROBERT opens the envelope and pulls out the small stack of pages.*

I should like to call it *Refuse Really* or *Satan on My Back* but I settled on *The Seven Pillars of Wisdom; A Triumph*. It's a complete fraud, a joke really.

ROBERT   Chapters 1 through 4?

NED   And the address of a publisher in the United States. They might be interested in printing it serially.

ROBERT   You want me to publish this for you?

NED   And I want you to accept the royalties. I'm afraid there is no use protesting, for I am determined to make not a farthing from the war. You might as well have it.

ROBERT   I don't want it.

NED   Consider it a reward.

ROBERT   What for?

NED   For bringing about the early retirement of Lord Curzon. Winston Churchill has dissolved his Middle East Department. It seems I am to ride again. I'm going to put the Emir Feisal in charge of Mesopotamia and rechristen the whole thing the Kingdom of Iraq. The Oxford Roof Climbers' Rebellion was not a complete failure.

ROBERT   I must tell you I am not a standing member of the Oxford Roof Climbers, The Benevolent Order of.

> *ROBERT places the envelope and stack of pages on the table.*

NED   I should think that after all you've been through, you've earned your membership, if you would like it.

ROBERT   After everything I've been through I should think I've also earned the right to refuse my membership.

NED   Do you refuse?

ROBERT   I do.

NED   There's a lovely newsletter?

ROBERT   No, thank you.

NED   I suppose then, that I am the heir of a long line of innocents. The last of the naïve. The final number of the futile. The Oxford Roof Climber's Rebellion? Me, myself and I.

ROBERT   A camel charge of one.

NED   I do believe it's my favourite kind.

ROBERT   You do so love being a martyr.

NED   You've got me wrong, Robert. I do so hate sharing the glory of victory. Keep the book anyway, if might be good for something really helpful, like paying the rent.

From the laundry on the table, NED places two small pairs of baby socks on the envelope and stack of pages.

ROBERT   Tell us your story.

NED   Which?

NANCY   About dining with Auda Abu Tayi in Prince Feisal's tent.

NED   Ah yes, are you sure you want to hear it? All right then, but tell me if I've heard this one before. Auda was sitting there with his legs crossed, eating with one hand, when suddenly he gave a great shout and stormed out of the tent. Feisal and I and the others followed him out to see what had so alarmed him. Auda, very agitated, spat out his false teeth and smashed them into bits upon a rock with his boot and rifle butt. Then with his toothless mouth he kissed Feisal's hand over and over, begging his pardon and professing his shame.

NANCY   Why would he do such a thing to his teeth?

NED   Auda had realized that he was dining with a descendant of the prophet Mohammed, peace be upon him, with false teeth that were a gift of a Turkish General. He spent the rest of the Arab Revolt toothless and some days when he ate I could see his intense pain. I'd tease him if today was the day he regretted smashing his teeth? And he told me that for a wise man I had much to learn… the pain today, and the pain yesterday, and the pain tomorrow reminded him of love. The pain you see, was everything. And then he said *El Aurens, imuhimm nlaa'i maHall naZiff, w'akil Tayyib.*

NANCY   And that means?

NED   He said I troubled him like women. And now, I have a train to catch only this time I'm going to be a passenger.

ROBERT   You have something more to say.

NED   There are many, many things and at the heart of them, there is one thing and… I couldn't bear to trouble you with it.

ROBERT   I see. A terrible pity.

NED   Yes, that's me all right. Oh, one last thing, I must confess that my story about Auda's teeth may not be entirely the truth. My Arabic translation was not accurate. *Imuhimm nlaa'i maHall naZiff, w'akil Tayyib* means "the important thing is to find a clean place and good food."

> *LAWRENCE bows in the Arab fashion, which he finishes with the salute of Oxford Roof Climbers, the Benevolent Order of. He then exits. ROBERT steps to the door to watch him go and then turns to face his wife. NANCY picks up a pair of the baby socks from NED's manuscript.*
>
> *The End.*

•STEPHEN MASSICOTTE•

Stephen's award winning plays *A Farewell to Kings, Pervert (The Dirty/Beautiful), The Emperor of Atlantis* and the popular "Star Wars" inspired *Boy's Own Jedi Handbook* series have played for audiences throughout Canada. In 2002 his play *Mary's Wedding* premiered at Alberta Theatre Projects' annual playRites Festival and was the winner of the 2000 Alberta Playwriting Competition, the 2002 Betty Mitchell Award for Best New Play and the 2003 Alberta Book Award for Drama. *Mary's Wedding* continues to be produced in English and French throughout Canada, the UK and the US. His film writing credits include the screenplays for the feature films "Ginger Snaps Back: The Beginning" and "The Dark." Stephen has a BFA in Drama from the University of Calgary and a black lab named Agnes. For more information see: www.stephenmassicotte.com.